DOLPHIN MAN

Exploring the World of Dolphins

LAURENCE PRINGLE

PHOTOGRAPHS BY
RANDALL S. WELLS
AND
CHICAGO ZOOLOGICAL
SOCIETY

BOYDS MILLS PRESS

For Rebecca, who prompts us all to say, "I love you."
—L. P.

To my parents, Fran and Jack, for teaching me to care
about the lives of other creatures, and for giving me the freedom
and encouragement to pursue my dreams.
—R. S. W.

Text copyright © 1995 by Laurence Pringle
Photographs copyright © 1995 by Randall S. Wells and Chicago Zoological Society

Published by Boyds Mills Press, Inc.
A Highlights Company
815 Church Street
Honesdale, Pennsylvania 18431
Printed in China
Visit our Web site at www.boydsmillspress.com

Publisher Cataloging-in-Publication Data

Pringle, Laurence.
   Dolphin man : exploring the world of dolphins / by Laurence Pringle :
photographs by Randall S. Wells : Chicago Zoological Society, 1st ed.
[48] p. : col. photo. ;   cm.
Includes index.
Originally published : New York: Atheneum, 1995. Books for Young Readers: An imprint of Simon & Schuster
Summary: A biography of marine biologist Randall S. Wells and his studies of bottlenose dolphins
in Sarasota Bay, Florida.
ISBN 1-59078-004-3
1. Dolphins—Pictorial works—Juvenile literature. (1. Dolphins—Pictorial works.)
I. Wells, Randall S. II. Chicago Zoological Society. III. Title.
599.53 21   CIP   QL737.C432   2002
2001093640

First Boyds Mills Press paperback edition, 2002
The text of this book is set in 13-point Garamond Book.

10 9 8 7 6 5 4 3

DOLPHIN MAN

CONTENTS

When dolphins rise to breathe, they often can be identified by distinctive marks on their dorsal fins.

ONE

Becoming Dolphin Man

"Dolphin at ten o'clock!" yelled a volunteer.

Randy Wells quickly cut the boat's speed and turned its bow westward. He and the rest of his crew scanned the water's surface, watching for the dolphins' next rise. A half minute passed. No dolphins in sight.

The seconds ticked away. Still nothing. Then suddenly dolphins rose to the surface in groups of two and three on both sides of the boat. For an instant each dolphin revealed the top of its head and body, including its big dorsal (back) fin, before diving under again. And in that instant Randy Wells began to call out their names:

"Pumpkin . . . Lightning . . . Merrily! And there's 55!"

In another half minute the dolphins rose to breathe again. "There's 75 and her calf, and Killer and her calf," Randy called. Soon he had identified four more dolphins for a total of a dozen— about a tenth of the bottlenose dolphins that live in Sarasota Bay on Florida's central western coast.

The boat followed the dolphins slowly as crew members took photographs of them and wrote down notes about their location

Notes are taken about each dolphin's identity, location, and behavior.

and behavior. Randy and his crew discussed the identity of each dolphin, trying to make sure that they were correct.

The photographs they took were not casual snapshots. Each year the research team led by Randy Wells takes twenty thousand photos of dolphins to record marks on their dorsal fins and other distinctive features that are clues to their identification. During some years they also capture some of the dolphins in nets to briefly study them more closely, and to collect blood samples and other information before they release them.

Getting to know more than a hundred dolphins is much more difficult than observing individual land animals. Biologists who study such mammals as wild jackals, lions, and chimpanzees, for example, can often sit and watch known individuals go about their daily lives in full view. The lives of dolphins are mostly hidden underwater. However, a great deal has been learned about the lives of the dolphin community of Sarasota Bay, thanks to the cooperative efforts of Randy Wells and other scientists, and help contributed by hundreds of volunteers.

"When I was a child," Randy says, "I never dreamed I would someday be studying dolphins, but my interest in ocean life began early."

Randall S. Wells was born in 1953, in Peoria, Illinois, about 750 miles from the nearest wild dolphins. When he was four years old, his parents took him on a two-week vacation on Florida's Gulf Coast. They all loved the area, and this vacation became an annual event.

"I became more and more fascinated by the sea, by its mysteries. It was like a Christmas present, with something unknown beneath the wrapping. I would stare at the water's surface and wonder what lay below."

By the time Randy was in junior high school, his interest in marine biology and oceanography really took hold. His science fair projects featured these subjects. He read books about marine life by Jacques Cousteau and others. He watched the then-popular television show about a dolphin, "Flipper." Early in his teenage years, however, he was more interested in sharks than in dolphins.

Randy's parents were also drawn to the ocean, and in 1969 the Wells family moved to Siesta Key, which is part of Sarasota. Siesta Key was then the location of the Mote Marine Laboratory, a private, nonprofit research lab where biologists study sharks, dolphins, sea turtles, and the other marine life of the southwest Florida coast.

That fall Randy started his junior year at Riverview High School, where he was delighted to find courses in marine ecology and oceanography. He began thinking he might be able to find a career studying marine life. Randy recalls that his parents always encouraged him to pursue his interests—and to work hard. They said, "Be a garbage collector if you want, but be the best garbage collector you can be."

Randy, then sixteen years old, tried to get a job for the next summer vacation at the Mote Marine Laboratory. "I volunteered to

By age 13, Randy Wells was fascinated with ocean life. He is shown here rescuing a shark cast ashore by a fisherman.

do tank cleaning or any kind of work, but there were no openings."

Then some serendipity—unplanned good fortune—touched Randy's life. A biologist named Blair Irvine joined the staff of Mote Marine Lab. While looking for a house, he met Randy's father, who was in the real estate business. Mr. Wells told Blair Irvine about Randy's strong interest in sea life. As a result, that summer Randy became a volunteer at the Mote Laboratory. All through his senior year of high school, he continued as a paid part-time worker on Blair Irvine's projects.

The work was not glamorous, and some of it was boring. Randy cleaned the large tanks (pools) in which animals were kept, chopped the fish that was their food, and recorded data. However, he loved working with the animals. The lab had been funded by the Office of Naval Research to learn whether dolphins could be trained to drive sharks away from people in the water. A captive bottlenose dolphin named Simo was trained to rush at a shark, or even to ram its beak (rostrum) into the gill area of a shark, in order to repel it.

Then, one at a time, sharks of different species were released in the large tank where Simo lived. At the sound of the attack signal—underwater "pings"—Simo chased away brown, lemon, and nurse sharks. These were promising results, but Blair Irvine had deliberately chosen to start with shark species that are not usually a threat to humans or dolphins.

The crucial part of the study came when a more dangerous species, the bull shark, was put in Simo's pool. Simo swam away, looking over his shoulder at the shark. He didn't respond to the attack signal. The shark was quickly removed from the tank, but two days passed before Simo returned to normal behavior. A second trial had the same results. Bull sharks attack dolphins, and Simo had instantly recognized one of his natural enemies.

Randy was 16 when he trained the dolphin Simo at Mote Marine Laboratory.

Eventually Simo was released in the place where he had been captured. After working with both sharks and Simo, Randy Wells felt a growing curiosity about the lives of wild dolphins. Even before the experiments with Simo concluded, Randy helped launch a dolphin study that continues to this day. He was just sixteen years old.

"In 1970," says Randy Wells, "most of what people knew about dolphins had been learned from captive animals. Blair Irvine wanted to answer some questions about wild dolphins. For example, we didn't know whether the bottlenose dolphins in Sarasota Bay stayed in that area or roamed all over the west coast of Florida. To answer that question, we had to begin marking individual dolphins so they could be recognized in the wild."

A large net and a large crew are needed to catch wild dolphins. Blair Irvine and Randy Wells could not manage it alone. Beginning in 1970, however, Blair obtained the cooperation of local commercial dolphin catchers who netted a few each year to supply oceanariums, marine life tourist attractions, and other buyers. The commercial netters wanted young, unscarred female dolphins, but they caught both males and females, old and young, and this gave the researchers opportunities to examine and mark the dolphins that were being returned to the water.

Through trail and error they learned that tags often did not stay attached to the dorsal fins of dolphins. However, the scar left by a missing tag could be an aid to identification. Blair and Randy also began putting freeze brands on the backs of dolphins at the base of their dorsal finds. (To freeze-brand a dolphin, metal numbers are supercooled in liquid nitrogen, then held against the dolphin's skin for fifteen seconds. This harmless technique causes the skin's gray pigment to move away from the surface, leaving the shape of the numbers in white.) These scars and brands served also to protect the dolphins from being kept by commercial collectors.

By the time Randy Wells graduated from Riverview High School, he had helped mark and release several bottlenose dolphins caught in Sarasota Bay. He continued to help Blair Irvine that summer, and even on vacations from the University of South Florida in Tampa, where he began to study zoology in the fall of 1971.

"Though I didn't know it at the time," Randy recalls, "some of the dolphins I handled and helped name—Granny, Melba, Nat—would be part of my life for many years to come."

TWO

Getting to Know Dolphins, One by One

Dolphins are among the most intelligent mammals on earth. They adapt quickly to new situations, and in captivity can be taught all sorts of complicated behaviors. The bottlenose dolphin is the species people usually see performing at aquariums and on television.

Bottlenoses are one of about thirty-two species of dolphins worldwide. All dolphins are toothed whales. The few species that are called porpoises have spade-shaped teeth and blunt, rounded faces. True dolphins have teeth shaped like rounded cones set in jaws that extend in a snout or beak.

The biggest dolphin is the killer whale, which may grow to be thirty-two feet long. The smallest, just five feet long, is the tucuxi that lives in the freshwater Amazon River and brackish coastal waters of South America. Even among the bottlenose species there is a size range. The biggest bottlenoses, found in the cold Atlantic waters off Scotland, grow to be thirteen feet long and may weigh a thousand pounds. Those that live along the coastal United States measure up to nine feet long, with the big males weighing six hundred pounds.

Dolphins could easily kill people, but they do not. Even when Randy Wells and a dozen or more helpers enclose dolphins in a net corral, they do not harm the people in the water. Why, then, is one Sarasota Bay dolphin named Killer? Randy explains: "When a dolphin is first captured, it may put up some resistance, but Killer's behavior during her first capture in 1975 was remarkable. She never calmed down. Even after she was held on a stretcher in the water, she managed to drag eight people and three boats around. No one was hurt. We named her Killer as a tribute to her feistiness. Today, Killer is as docile as any other animal we handle, but her kids show some of the same feistiness."

After grasping a fish in its teeth, a dolphin often swallows it whole.

This dolphin caught a mullet by its tail.

Dolphin teeth are used for grasping, not chewing. They have no jaw muscles for chewing. A dolphin grabs its prey, then swallows it whole, or rubs it against the bottom or whacks it on the water surface to break it into chunks that can be swallowed. Dolphin diets, and their feeding behavior, vary with their habitat. The species that live mostly in rivers hunt alone and catch fish and crustaceans. In contrast, dolphins that live in the open ocean may hunt in cooperative groups. They surround and "herd" schools of fish or squid, maneuvering them into position for attack.

Dolphins living along coasts are opportunistic feeders. They take advantage of whatever food is available, depending on the habitat and the season. They sometimes encounter schools of fish and use teamwork to catch some. Mostly, however, they hunt for individual fish. A large male or a female bottlenose dolphin nursing a calf may eat as many as thirty pounds of fish a day.

In the summer, fish called mullet are abundant in Sarasota Bay.

Mullet frequently leap out of the water. Sometimes, however, you may see a mullet go tumbling high and far through the air. Randy Wells explains why:

"Pursued by a dolphin, a fish often tries to evade capture by abruptly changing direction. To counter this ploy, the mammal whirls and swats its victim with its broad flukes. The blow is power ful enough to stun or kill the fish and occasionally sends it flying. Then the 'fishwhacking' dolphin swims over to collect its catch."

In Sarasota Bay dolphins also eat pinfish, pigfish, and catfish. Researchers following dolphin schools sometimes find numerous front halves of catfish at the surface. The dolphins eat the tail ends

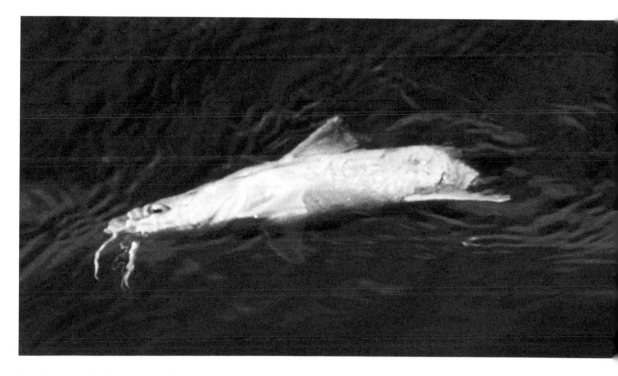

By biting off the tail end of a catfish, a dolphin avoids sharp spines located just behind the fish's head.

and avoid the dangerous barbs that protrude just behind the catfish heads.

After just a few years of marking dolphins and watching for known individuals, Randy Wells and Blair Irvine saw evidence that the dolphins stayed in the Sarasota Bay area. The bay was a natural laboratory for research on a population of dolphins, and Randy was curious to know more about the lives of those he knew by sight. However, funds weren't then available for a major dolphin study.

On vacations from college Randy continued to be Blair Irvine's research assistant, and he is grateful for those early experiences: "One of the first things Blair asked me to do as a high school volunteer was build a box of wood and fiberglass for storing some equipment; I still use that box. I was asked to do a lot of basic stuff, like painting and repairs. I learned to fix whatever was broken, take care of boats. Colleges don't usually teach such things, but biologists who work outdoors need to have these skills."

After graduating from the University of South Florida in 1975, Randy began studying for a master's degree in zoology at the University of Florida in Gainesville. His subject: the Atlantic bottlenose dolphins of the west coast of Florida.

Following passage of the Marine Mammal Protection Act of 1972, government agencies encouraged more research on dolphins, other whales, and manatees. Beginning in 1974, the U.S. Marine Mammal Commission provided funds for further study of dolphins in the Sarasota Bay area.

Michael Scott joined Blair Irvine and Randy Wells in an effort to capture, mark, and release more dolphins. From January 1975 through July 1976, they caught and tagged forty-seven bottlenose dolphins. They equipped ten dolphins with radio transmitters and tracked their movements for up to three weeks.

About a hundred bottlenose dolphins live in the Sarasota Bay area. Their range includes the southern edge of Tampa Bay and extends into the Gulf of Mexico.

Tagging a dolphin in 1976 were, left to right, Blair Irvine, Randy Wells, and Michael Scott.

The results of the radio-tracking studies and sightings of marked dolphins suggested that about a hundred animals live year-round in the Sarasota Bay area. To the north their home range includes the southern edge of Tampa Bay. To the west it extends a mile or so into the Gulf of Mexico.

With regret, Randy had to leave this community of dolphins for a while. He wanted to earn a doctorate degree, and that goal took him far from Florida to do research on other kinds of whales or cetaceans (the scientific name of whales; the name comes from the Greek word ketos, which means "big fish").

The first step toward that goal occurred in 1976, when Randy accidentally met Dr. Kenneth Norris, a world renowned whale researcher from the University of California at Santa Cruz. In August of that year, they met on a sailing ship off Newfoundland,

Blair Irvine releases a dolphin after attaching a radio transmitter to its dorsal fin. The transmitter released automatically in about two weeks.

when Randy was assisting a study of humpback whales. Ken Norris was impressed with the young biologist from Florida. The following summer he called Randy and asked him to join a research project on spinner dolphins.

After completing work at the University of Florida in 1978, Randy began his studies at the University of California. He spent much of the next two and a half years in Hawaii, where as many as nine researchers studied the behavior of spinner dolphins, which live in schools of up to 250 animals. Randy worked on many aspects of the study, which included radio tracking, recording dolphin sounds, and observations from cliffs, aircraft, and large and small vessels, including a glass-bottomed boat for watching underwater behavior.

At one time or another Randy did all of these things. "I learned a lot," he recalls, "and sometimes thought of how some techniques could be used in Sarasota Bay. I saw how more extensive use of

Spinner dolphins rise to the surface in the clear Pacific waters off Hawaii. Using a glass bottom boat, Ken Norris (at the helm), Randy Wells, and other researchers were able to watch the underwater behavior of these dolphins.

photos could help identify additional dolphins and wanted to try that back home."

In 1981, his Hawaiian fieldwork completed, Randy continued in Santa Cruz, preparing the part of his doctoral degree thesis that was on spinner dolphins and helping Ken Norris with other projects. Randy also conducted studies of blue whales off the California coast. Other research projects took him to the Beaufort Sea in the Arctic to study bowhead whales and to the Bering Sea off Alaska to study gray whales.

"Many good things happened during those years in California," Randy says, "and they were not all related to learning about whales. In 1985 I met Michelle Jeffries, a marine biologist who had cared for and studied sea lions at the Long Marine Lab and later worked there as Ken Norris's head dolphin trainer. Michelle and I were married in 1989."

Although he spent most of the 1980s in California, Randy never lost touch with the bottlenose dolphins of Sarasota Bay, nor with researchers there. In 1982 he joined Blair Irvine and Michael Scott to form the Dolphin Biology Research Institute. Establishing this nonprofit institute helped them to get funds and equipment—including donated boats—to continue long-term studies of bottlenose dolphins.

By early 1984 a total of 466 bottlenose dolphins had been photographed along the western Florida coast, including areas north and south of Sarasota Bay. In the bay itself the numbers stayed at about a hundred, and most of the dolphins known from the 1970s were still living there in the 1980s.

In 1984, Randy Wells and his fellow researchers began a new effort to learn more about these dolphins. The program continues today. For about ten days during certain years they briefly capture some of the Sarasota Bay dolphins in order to learn the sex, age, and identity of every resident of the dolphin community, and to check on the health of animals already identified. A wealth of other information is gathered before the dolphins are released unharmed.

Catching and working with wild dolphins is possible in Sarasota Bay because the animals can be encircled over sea-grass meadows where the water is shallow enough for people to stand. Nevertheless, catching small groups of dolphins is a big job. It requires several boats and at least thirty people. Some are scientists who are there to gather different kinds of information. They fly in from Woods Hole Oceanographic Institution in Massachusetts, from the University of California at Santa Cruz, from the National Marine Fisheries Service, and from Portland State University in Oregon.

Others are needed to handle the big, powerful dolphins. Students from colleges in the Sarasota area have helped, as have volunteers from the Earthwatch Institute, an organization whose citizen-members supports all sorts of scientific research.

"We get an early start," explains Randy, "to avoid being chased off the water by one of those thunder and lightning storms that are so common on Florida afternoons. First we locate a specific group of dolphins. We don't disturb the community's oldest animals or mothers with young calves. Then a commercial fishing boat encircles the dolphins with a 1,500-foot net. One by one, each dolphin is maneuvered onto a sling that is lifted out of the water so the animal can be weighed. Then the dolphin is placed on the deck of the boat that serves as our floating veterinary laboratory.

"Each animal is out of the water for no more than an hour. Some volunteers gather around the dolphin and help by shading its eyes from the sun and by keeping its skin moist. The scientific members of the team quickly gather all sorts of information. For example, if the dolphin is one whose age is unknown, a veterinarian gives it a local anesthetic in its lower jaw and removes a tooth. Later on, study of the growth rings in the tooth will reveal the animal's age. The dolphin is given a freeze-brand mark, and photos are taken of fins and scars so it can be recognized again.

"We check the body condition of each animal by taking many measurements, including the thickness of its blubber. This is done by ultrasound—using sound wave reflections to get a picture of the blubber. Blood samples are taken. From them we can learn a great deal about the dolphin's health, including the amounts of pesticides and other pollutants it carries. We can even learn the identity of its mother and father.

After dolphins are encircled with a net, volunteers help researchers measure and weigh the animals. They also monitor their breathing patterns and heartbeats.

By temporarily attaching a microphone in a soft rubber suction cup to the dolphin's melon, researchers were able to record its individual whistle.

"Our capture-release program also gives us an opportunity to record each dolphin's 'personalized' signature whistle. We do this by placing a suction cup containing a small underwater microphone on the animal's 'melon,' the foreheadlike bulge between its beak and blowhole. The microphone is linked to a tape recorder by a long cable."

The dolphins usually remain quite docile while in the net corral. Those that have been captured before put up the least resistance. A few dolphins that have been caught several times swim right up to volunteers in the water and solicit petting.

The dolphins are soon freed from the net corral, leaving the scientists with a tremendous amount of information that may take months to analyze. These capture-release efforts last only a few weeks a year, but they eventually produce fascinating details about individual dolphins and how they are related to others in their community.

After a wealth of information has been gathered, the dolphins are freed and swim away.

THREE

Growing Up in a Dolphin Community

People are often amazed when Randy Wells swiftly names dolphins as they flash to the surface, then disappear underwater. Of course, a few dolphins are easy to identify. There's Half Mast, who lost a big chunk of her dorsal fin to a shark. Rip Torn has distinctive scars from a boat's propeller. And the top half of Sparks's dorsal fin is tipped to one side.

At first glance the rest all seem alike. When you look more closely, however, you begin to see distinctive marks, especially on the trailing edge of their dorsal fins. If you study photos of the patterns of nicks and notches, the differences among dolphins become clearer. This ability to identify specific animals, combined with information gained by catching them, has enabled Randy and other researchers to learn a lot about the Sarasota Bay bottlenose dolphin community.

The dolphin Rip Torn (top right) is named for wounds left by a boat propeller, while Shark Bait (center) has wounds from a shark attack. The dorsal fin of a dolphin named Otter (bottom) has less noticeable marks.

A dolphin calf stays close to its mother's side.

Randy calls it a dolphin "community" rather than a "population" because some of the dolphins do leave their forty-eight-square-mile home range. One male, called 154, wasn't seen in the bay for eight years, then returned. Males from Sarasota Bay have been seen visiting other areas, including Tampa Bay to the north. And genetic information from blood samples shows that Sarasota Bay females breed with males from other dolphin communities.

At the core of the Sarasota Bay community are mother dolphins and their calves. They form strong bonds and swim in the largest groups. Three generations of females have been observed within a single group.

Most calves are born from May through July, when the water

temperature may reach eighty-five degrees Fahrenheit or more. The timing is important, since a newborn calf has very little blubber to insulate it from cold. It might not survive birth in winter, when temperatures may drop below fifty-five degrees Fahrenheit.

The instant a calf is born, its mother spins away from it, snapping the umbilical cord. Then the calf swims to the surface for its first breath. It weighs about thirty pounds. Its dark skin is temporarily marked with creases and stripes that show how the calf was folded up in its mother's womb. Like all mammals, dolphin mothers give their young milk. Within a few hours of birth, the calf learns to nurse, taking quick bursts of rich milk several times each hour.

Little dolphins usually nurse from their mothers for several years, though they start to eat fish within six months of birth. In a Natural History magazine article entitled "Bringing Up Baby" Randy Wells wrote, "The young dolphins play 'cat and mouse' games with small fish such as pinfish, catching them with their teeth, throwing them, and allowing them to swim off a short distance before recapturing them and continuing the game."

Dolphin calves are always close to their mothers. Nevertheless, some of them die—from disease, shark bites, or other, unknown causes. It seems that a female dolphin has to learn how to be a good mother. A female's first and second calves often don't survive. The older, more experienced females are usually more successful in raising their calves until they can live independently.

Randy Wells wrote: "Losing an infant appears to be stressful for the mother. . . . Saida Beth's first calf died within one day of birth. After the death, we found Saida Beth with ten other dolphins, including three mother-calf pairs and her own mother, Melba, traveling slowly north over a sea-grass meadow. . . . While we watched, the rest of the group continued north, but Saida and Melba remained. Saida circled in a highly agitated manner, lifting her dead

Hannah's calf died soon after receiving this massive shark bite.

son to the surface, whistling, dropping the calf, then repeating the process every few minutes."

Saida Beth tried to revive her son for another hour and a half. Then she was chased from the area by two rowdy teenage male dolphins and did not return.

Young calves that survive birth spend much of their early lives in sea-grass nursery areas where the water is only a few feet deep. Sometimes a group of mothers form a half-circle "playpen" where their young can play safely. A mother and calf swim together, side by side, for an average period of five and a half years. Sometimes a calf leaves just before the birth of its mother's next calf, but in a few cases the older calf remains with its mother following the arrival of a new calf.

"Young dolphins benefit in many ways from this close relation-ship with their mothers," says Randy Wells. "They form lifelong bonds with other members of mother-calf groups. They are given protection. Danger, in the form of several species of large, predatory sharks, lurks in the deeper waters of the dolphins' home range. Dolphin calves also learn their way around that range.

"One day, Merrily, Granny's nine-month-old daughter, got tangled in a fishing net near the northern extreme of the range. We removed and held her, hoping that Granny would come looking for her, but a thunderstorm forced us to send her on her own. Hours later we found the young dolphin in her mother's familiar waters four miles to the south, and by the next day she and Granny were together."

Calves do eventually leave their mothers but may stay in touch for the rest of their lives. The birth of a new calf, for example, often results in visits from the mother's other offspring. Also, Randy Wells reported in 1991: "We have observed baby-sitting by older sisters, by other band members, and in one case, by Puka Fin, at thirty-nine

Mother dolphins and their calves travel and rest together.

Subadult or "juvenile' dolphins play and socialize a lot.

years of age the oldest known-age male in the community. From our genetic studies we discovered that he may have been the father of two of the three youngsters in the group."

When a calf does finally leave its mother, it joins a subadult group of both males and females. They range in age from about three to thirteen years. These dolphins behave somewhat like human teenagers. They are very active—leaping, chasing, and socializing. There is some rough play, with bites and tail slaps. The dolphins may be establishing who is dominant to whom.

Female dolphins usually have their first calf when they are between eight and twelve years of age. Males begin to breed when they reach their maximum size, at thirteen to twenty years of age.

The males stay with subadult groups until they are ten to fifteen years old. During this period they form long-lasting bonds with other males that may continue the rest of their lives. Male pairs often swim close to each other and even rise to the surface to breathe at the same instant.

"The death of one of these males must be quite a blow to the survivor," says Randy. "The buddy of the dolphin we call 44 disappeared. And Kid lost his buddy, Nat, to disease. For a time we saw Kid team up with other males. Finally he and 44 began to hang out together. They formed a strong bond and are now together all the time. Interestingly, both Kid and 44 were once members of the same subadult group."

Dolphins sometimes leap several feet above the water as they play and interact with other dolphins.

There are a few lone males in the Sarasota dolphin community, and one lone female, Hannah. She has not been able to successfully raise a calf. In 1989 a shark killed her most recent calf when it was five months old. Living in pairs or in larger groups probably helps dolphins survive. One animal can rest while another is vigilant. Dolphins and other whales cannot sleep as most other mammals do; they have to rise to breathe every half minute or so. However, they rest by "shutting down" half of their brain and not using the echolocation system that helps them detect approaching danger.

For dolphins of the Sarasota Bay community, that danger is sharks. Not counting young calves, nearly 31 percent of the dolphins have shark scars. However, Randy Wells believes that most adult dolphins survive shark attacks. A healthy dolphin is probably powerful enough to lunge away before a shark's teeth cut through its blubber layer and reach muscle. "Blubber," explains Randy, "is a form of armor as well as an insulator and energy store."

The bottlenose dolphins may face their greatest threat from sharks in the fall or winter, when their main source of food, mullet, form schools and swim through inlets and out into the Gulf of Mexico to spawn. The dolphins follow partway, spending more time in the inlets and gulf, where the water is deep and where tiger, dusky, and bull sharks may lurk.

In recent years, Randy reports, the threat of sharks has declined. Overfishing has caused their numbers to drop along the western coast of Florida (and all over the world). However, this isn't necessarily good news for dolphins. Sharks commonly also feed on their relatives, the stingrays, and it appears that rays have become more plentiful as shark numbers have declined. Increasing numbers of dolphins are being harmed from encounters with rays.

When a dolphin accidentally swims close to a stingray hidden on the bottom, the ray defends itself with its barbed sting.

Stabbed with a broken-off sting, a dolphin may die as the sting works inward through its muscles and into its organs. Several bottlenose dolphins found dead along the western Florida coast died this way.

In western Florida, many dolphins, other whales, and manatees found dead or alive on the shore are reported to the Mote Marine Laboratory. It has researchers and facilities for studying dead marine mammals and trying to rescue live ones. Through all of his years in California, Randy Wells kept in touch with the staff at the Mote Laboratory.

In 1989 Randy became a conservation biologist for the Chicago Zoological Society at the Brookfield Zoo. Michelle Wells also joined the zoo as an animal keeper working with dolphins, seals, sea lions, and walrus. Randy continued to focus his attention on bottlenose dolphins. The Chicago Zoological Society supported much of his research in Florida, and Randy found himself spending more and more time in Sarasota. He launched new studies of dolphins in Florida and advised young researchers.

In 1992 the Wellses moved to Sarasota, because the Chicago Zoological Society allowed Randy to establish his research base there. For about a year Michelle was manager of Randy's ever-growing information about dolphins, setting up a computer database for it. Then she returned to her career as an animal trainer and became responsible for animal care for Mote Marine Lab's Marine Mammal Stranding Program.

Randy's years of experience with dolphins and whales were valued by the Mote Laboratory, and in 1992, in a cooperative effort with the Chicago Zoological Society, he was named manager of its Marine Mammal Research Program. In exchange for this work, his office and staff are now headquartered at Mote Marine Laboratory.

The office windows have a view of Sarasota Bay, and sometimes of leaping dolphins.

FOUR

For Dolphins Everywhere

With its eyes covered, a dolphin can navigate and find small objects by listening to echoes of clicks it emits. In 1988 researchers at California's Long Marine Laboratory wanted to learn more about the workings of this remarkable echolocation system. For their studies they needed two bottlenose dolphins. Ken Norris and Randy Wells recognized this as an opportunity to answer a question: Can dolphins that have been removed from the wild for a small fraction of their total life span be released back into their home waters and return successfully to their native society?

This project involved a lot of thought and planning before the dolphins were caught. Early on, one important question was: Which dolphins? Having observed the strong bonds that form between male dolphins, Ken Norris and Randy decided that two subadult males were the best candidates. They hoped the dolphins would develop a bond that would help them in captivity and continue after they were returned to the wild.

In July 1988 two male dolphins (one six years old, the other seven) were caught in Tampa Bay and flown to California.

Captured in Florida, Misha and Echo were flown to California for study at Long Marine Laboratory, and then were returned to their native Florida waters.

They were named Echo and Misha. Michelle was their head trainer, teaching them to perform for tests of their echolocation skills. Meanwhile, researchers in Florida made boat trips to the area where Echo and Misha had been netted in order to identify and observe the other dolphins there. Later on, when the dolphins were released, this information would help biologists judge how well they fit in.

Echo and Misha were flown back to Florida in the early fall of 1990. They were kept in a pen at Mote Marine Lab for three and a half weeks, fed local fish, and examined to make sure they were healthy. Then they were let go in the same area where they had been captured more than two years before. In the months that followed, a research team led by Randy's student, Kim Bassos-Hull, looked frequently for the two dolphins.

The bond that had developed in captivity was broken gradually, and then Echo and Misha went their separate ways. Nevertheless, the dolphins were healthy and interacting normally with other dolphins. One day in 1990, Michelle and Randy Wells found Echo swimming with other dolphins in Tampa Bay. The dolphins began "surfing" on the bow wave of their boat. Michelle blew several notes on the whistle that she had used to train Echo at Long Marine Lab in Santa Cruz. Echo responded with four leaps out of the water,

Michelle Wells trained Misha and Echo so that more could be learned about the echolocation skills of dolphins.

Echo leaped from the water and looked back when he heard the familiar sound of his training whistle.

turning his head to look back at Michelle. Then he returned to being a wild dolphin.

The two dolphins continued to lead healthy, normal lives. "This is encouraging," Randy said, "because dolphins are usually removed permanently from their communities when they are used for research or other purposes. Echo and Misha showed us that we sometimes have an alternative and can return dolphins to the waters and fellow dolphins they know so well."

Randy hopes the knowledge gained about the behavior of wild dolphin communities can lead to improved breeding programs for dolphins that are already captive. This would reduce the pressure to catch young animals from the wild—an act that interferes with

On weekends and holidays, the dolphins of Sarasota Bay must contend with noise and pollution from thousands of boats.

dolphin social systems and may even affect the survival of some dolphins that remain.

The well-being of Sarasota Bay's bottlenose dolphins, and of dolphins around the world, is one of Randy Wells's main concerns. He wondered whether the bay's dolphins are harmed by the thousands of boats and Jet Skis used there. Unlike manatees, dolphins usually avoid being hit by boats, but every Monday, after a busy boating weekend, the dolphins are wary and hard to approach. Dolphins rely on hearing to communicate, find food, and avoid harm, so Randy aims to find out whether "sound pollution" from boats interferes in a more serious way with their lives.

The Sarasota Bay dolphin community is clearly affected by loss of habitat. Shoreline development, dredging, and pollution have wiped out vast areas of sea-grass meadows. The dolphins mostly use the more northern areas, where the shoreline and underwater habitat is less disturbed.

Another concern is a buildup of pollutants, such as pesticide residues, in the bodies of dolphins. Some harmful chemicals are stored in blubber. A study of South African dolphins showed that nursing females passed 80 percent of these chemicals to their first born young, perhaps reducing their chances of survival. Samples of blood and milk from Florida dolphins are being tested for pollutants from their environments.

Bottlenose dolphins are commonly seen in parts of Sarasota Bay where the shoreline is still wild.

"We need to focus on health," Randy says, "to detect and treat problems before dolphins start washing up dead on the beach. Of course we are also trying to learn about the natural lives of wild dolphins, so questions arise about whether to interfere when a dolphin is stranded or injured. I'm not completely resolved about this, but humans do harm the dolphin community, so it seems right to compensate, to give some injured or sick dolphins a second chance."

Randy and his colleagues continue to survey dolphin communities beyond Sarasota Bay, north into Tampa Bay, south into Charlotte Harbor, and west into the Gulf of Mexico. By late 1994 they had identified by photos more than two thousand individual bottlenose dolphins. However, their main focus remained on the Sarasota Bay community—on its social structure, mating system, and communication system. In 1994 Randy worked with colleagues to begin the first field tests of a new lightweight radio-tracking system. Held on a dolphin by harmless suction cups, it has the potential to transmit information that includes the animal's location, depth, body temperature, heart rate, and swimming speed, as well as sounds sent and received.

When talking about dolphin research, Randy Wells emphasizes that when he says "I" he means "we." One person, working alone, could not learn much about wild dolphins. "This is such a team effort, with a dozen or more scientists from here and around the world, plus all of the volunteers. And the researchers benefit from the collaboration. The results of one study help others."

For example, when Peter Tyack of the Woods Hole Oceanographic Institution analyzes the dolphin whistles he records, he knows the age, sex, and other details about individual animals, thanks to Randy Wells's research. And when Aleta Hohn of the National Marine Fisheries Service works to perfect the technique of telling a dolphin's age by growth marks in its teeth, she too can use vital details from Randy's studies. The birth year of many Sarasota Bay dolphins is known from direct observation. This gives Aleta a standard by which to check the accuracy of the tooth growth mark technique. This method of telling the age of dolphins can be used not just on living dolphins but also on long-dead dolphins whose skulls—and teeth—are kept in museum collections all over the world.

The health and behavior of dolphins, their reproduction, the effects of pollution and boat traffic, on manatees as well as dolphins—all of these matters and more are being investigated by Randy Wells and other biologists. As director of Mote's Center for Marine Mammal and Sea Turtle Research, Randy has a fulltime staff of three biologists along with graduate students from the University of California at Santa Cruz, and Woods Hole Oceanographic Institution. At times the research requires help from as many as a dozen college student interns and volunteers from the Earthwatch Institute.

The passing years have brought changes in the lives of Sarasota Bay's dolphins, and in those of Randy and Michelle Wells, too. They are no longer together, though they remain good friends. Michelle is responsible for the care of the sea otters on display at the Monterey Bay Aquarium in California.

The year 2000 marked the thirtieth year of Randy Wells's research—the world's longest running dolphin study.

When Randy, Blair Irvine, and Michael Scott began their long-term studies, people believed that bottlenose dolphins lived about twenty-five years. They discovered that some dolphins reach old age at about forty to fifty years, and that females can bear calves in their late-forties.

Getting to know individual dolphins has rewarded Randy Wells both scientifically and personally. Some of the dolphins are old friends that Randy first met when he was a teenager. For Randy and his staff, the death of an old-timer feels like a death in the family.

Granny lived fifty years, and was probably a great-grandmother when she gave birth to this calf in 1989.

Melba was last seen alive in the summer of 1993, when she was fifty-two years old. In early 1994 Granny's body washed up on a beach. She had lived fifty years.

Randy says: "Granny's death didn't end her contribution to our dolphin research. We have blood and milk samples from her, collected several years ago, that will yield important information. And we are still studying three of her daughters, three grand-calves, along with great-grand-calves. From these four generations, and all the other Sarasota dolphins, we hope to learn things that will benefit dolphins everywhere."

FURTHER READING & WEB SITES

Connor, R. C., R. S. Wells, J. Mann, and A. J. Read. "The bottlenose dolphin, Tursiops spp: Social relationships in a fission-fusion society." In *Cetacean Societies: Field Studies of Dolphins and Whales,* J. Mann, R. C. Connor, P. L. Tyack, and H. Whitehead, eds., 91–126. Chicago: University of Chicago Press, 1999, 433 pp.

Norris, Kenneth S. *Dolphin Days: The Life and Times of the Spinner Dolphin.* New York: Avon, 1993.

———. "Dolphins in Crisis." *National Geographic* (September 1992): 2–35.

Reynolds, J. E. III, R. S. Wells, and S. D. Eide. *Biology and conservation of the bottlenose dolphin.* Gainesville, Fla.: University Press of Florida, 2000.

Wells, Randall S. "Bringing Up Baby." *Natural History* (August 1991): 56–62.

———. "The Marine Mammals of Sarasota Bay." Chapter 9 in *Sarasota Bay: Framework for Action.* Sarasota, Fla.: Sarasota Bay National Estuary Program, 1992.

———. "The Role of Long-Term Studies in Understanding the Social Structure of a Bottlenose Dolphin Community." In *Dolphin Societies: Discoveries and Puzzles,* K. Pryor and K. S. Norris, eds., 198–225. Berkeley and Los Angeles: University of California Press, 1991.

Wells, Randall S., Michael D. Scott, and A. Blair Irvine. "The Social Structure of Free-Ranging Bottlenose Dolphins." In *Current Mammalogy,* vol. 1. Edited by H. Genoways, 247–305. New York: Plenum Press, 1987.

Wells, R. S., D. J. Boness, and G. B. Rathbun. "Behavior." In *Biology of Marine Mammals,* J. E. Reynolds, III, and S. A. Rommel, eds., 324–422. Washington, D.C.: Smithsonian Institution Press, 1999, 578 pp.

WEB SITES:

Additional updated information on the Sarasota Dolphin Research Program can be found on the Brookfield Zoo Web site: www.brookfieldzoo.org, and the Mote Marine Laboratory Web site: www.mote.org.

INDEX